NEW & CREATI

ParacordCrafts

Ready for new paracord projects? How about jewelry with easy knot beads or other bling? Anyone on the go will want the shoulder-sling bottle holder, activists will love the support ribbons, and kids can have fun with the little "para-people."

2

4

6

9

10

14

16

19

19

LEISURE ARTS, INC. • Maumelle, Arkansas

Para Bling Bracelet

Approximate finished length: 7½"

SHOPPING LIST

- ☐ 7' length of paracord
- ☐ side-release buckle
- ☐ 4 metallic pony beads
- ☐ large-hole, metal-lined beads and spacers (1 really large bead or 2 smaller ones and 1 spacer)
- ☐ sharp scissors
- ☐ tape measure or ruler
- ☐ craft glue
- ☐ masking, painter's, or duct tape

To make the Bracelet:

Always apply craft glue to cut cord ends and allow to dry.

1. Cut an 18" length of cord.

2. Insert about 1" of the 18" cord length through one buckle piece from front to back. Secure the cord end with a narrow piece of tape *(Fig. 1)*.

   Fig. 1

   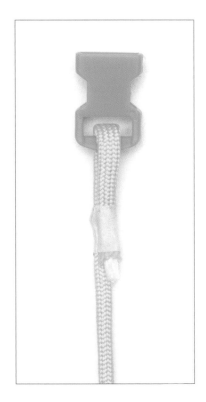

3. Fold the long cord in half and insert through the buckle from front to back. Bring the cord ends through the loop *(Fig. 2)*; pull to tighten. Tape the buckle down.

   Fig. 2

4. Use the long cords and follow Cobra Stitch Knot (page 22) to tie 3 Cobra Stitch Knots.

5. Slide a pony bead on the short cord and tie a Cobra Stitch Knot *(Fig. 3)*. Repeat once more.

   Fig. 3

   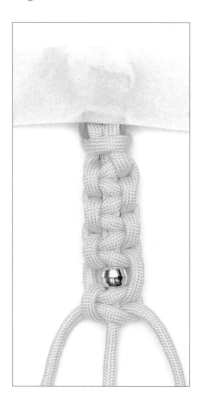

6. Slide the large-hole bead(s) on the short cord and tie a Cobra Stitch Knot. Slide on a pony bead and tie a knot. Slide on the last pony bead and tie 3 knots.

7. Follow Finishing The Ends (page 22) to complete the bracelet, threading the short cord under the last knot along with the long cords.

Loops & Bars Bracelet

To make the Bracelet:

Always apply craft glue to cut cord ends and allow to dry.

1. Measure your wrist and decide how loose you want your bracelet. This measurement is your finished bracelet size.

2. Fold the cords in half and insert the loops through one buckle piece from front to back. Bring the cords ends through the loops *(Fig. 1)* and pull to tighten.

Fig. 1

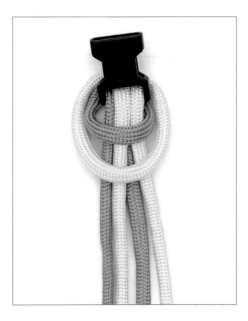

3. Arrange the cords as shown in Fig. 2. Tape down the buckle.

Fig. 2

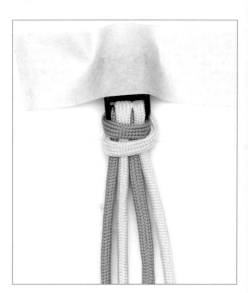

4. Loop the right outer cord under the two center cords and over the left outer cord *(Fig. 3)*.

Fig. 3

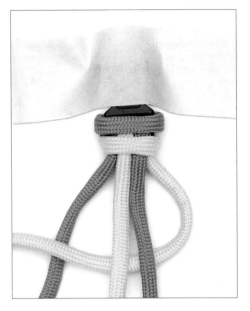

5. Loop the left outer cord over the left center cord, under the right outer cord, over the right center cord, and under the right loop *(Fig. 4)*.

Fig. 4

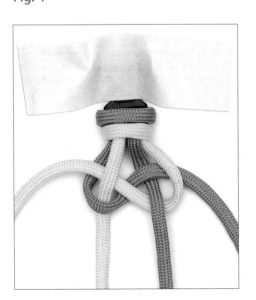

6. Loop the right outer cord over both center cords and under the left outer cord *(Fig. 5)*.

Fig. 5

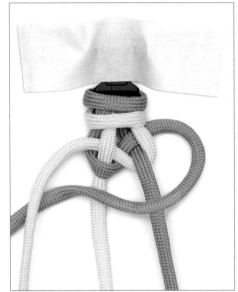

7. Loop the left outer cord under the left center cord, over the right outer cord, under the right center cord, and over the right loop *(Fig. 6)*; tighten slightly.

Fig. 6

8. Repeat Steps 4-7 until you reach your finished bracelet size.

9. Follow Cobra Stitch Knot (page 22) to tie a Cobra Stitch Knot with the outer cords around the center cords.

10. Working from front to back, insert all four cord ends through the remaining buckle piece.

11. Follow Finishing The Ends (page 22) to complete the bracelet, tucking all 4 cord ends under the last knot.

Para-People

SHOPPING LIST

Bead-Head Person

- [ ] 11" length of paracord (head and legs)
- [ ] 22" length of paracord (body and arms)
- [ ] 13mm large-hole wood bead
- [ ] sharp scissors
- [ ] tape measure or ruler
- [ ] craft glue
- [ ] masking, painter's, or duct tape

Knot-Head Person

- [ ] 26" length paracord (head and legs)
- [ ] 22" length of paracord (body and arms)
- [ ] sharp scissors
- [ ] tape measure or ruler
- [ ] craft glue
- [ ] masking, painter's, or duct tape

To make the Bead-Head Person:

Always apply craft glue to cut cord ends and allow to dry.

1. For the feet, tie an Overhand Knot (page 22) near each end of the 11" cord. Fold the cord in half (center cords). Center the 22" cord (outer cords) under the center cords, about 2¹/₂" from the fold *(Fig. 1)*.

Fig. 1

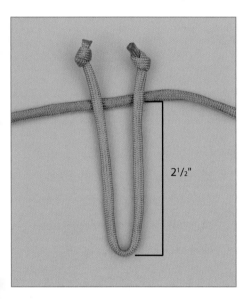

Tip:
You might find it helpful to tape down the feet for Steps 2 and 3, like we did in Figs. 7-8 on page 8.

2. For the body, use the outer cords to tie the first half of a Cobra Stitch Knot around the center cords *(Fig. 2)*; tighten *(Fig. 3)*.

Fig. 2

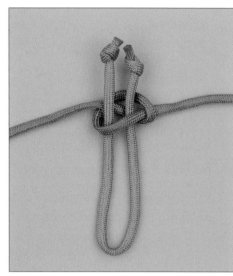

Fig. 3

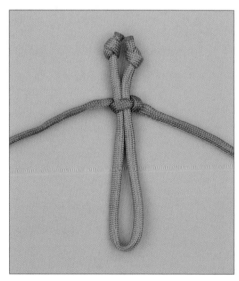

3. Tie the second half of a Cobra Stitch Knot around the center cords *(Fig. 4)*; tighten *(Fig. 5)*. Tie 2 more Cobra Stitch Knots.

Fig. 4

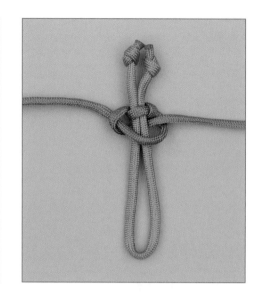

Fig. 5

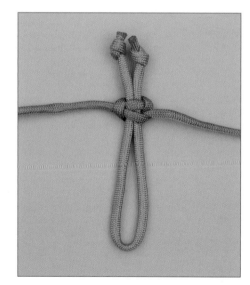

4. Turn the knotted piece around. Tie an Overhand Knot in each outer cord, about 1" away from the body. Trim the cord ends close to the knots. Slide the bead on the folded cord *(Fig. 6)*.

Fig. 6

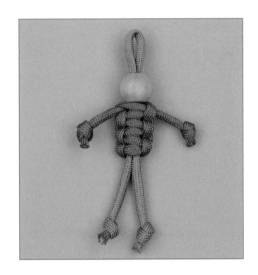

To make the Knot-Head Person:
Always apply craft glue to cut cord ends and allow to dry.

1. For the head, fold the 26" cord (center cords) in half.

2. Working about 1¹/₂" from the fold of the loop, tie a Diamond Knot (page 23) with the center cords. As you begin to tighten, you will need to keep adjusting the knot's loops so that the finished knot will stay about 1¹/₂" from the fold of the loop. When the knot is firm, pull both the loop and center cord ends to finish tightening.

3. For the body, position the center cords with the loop toward you; tape down the ends. Center the 22" cord (outer cords) under the center cords, about 2" from the Diamond Knot *(Fig. 7)*.

Fig. 7

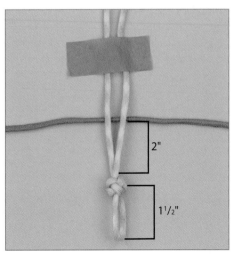

2"

1¹/₂"

4. Follow Steps 2-3 of Bead-Head Person (page 7) to tie 3 Cobra Stitch Knots with the outer cords around the center cords. Slide the Cobra Stitch Knots close to the Diamond Knot, if needed *(Fig. 8)*.

Fig. 8

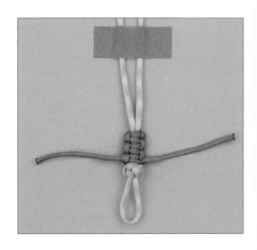

5. For the arms, tie an Overhand Knot (page 22) in each outer cord about 1" away from the body. Trim the outer cord ends close to the knots *(Fig. 9)*.

Fig. 9

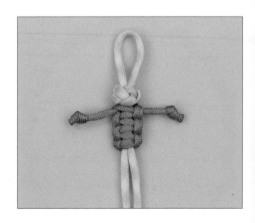

6. For the legs and feet, repeat Step 5, tying the Overhand Knots about 1¹/₂" below the body.

Beaded Single Strand Bracelet

SHOPPING LIST

- [ ] 12" length of paracord
- [ ] assorted beads (we used wood, metal, and plastic beads)
- [ ] 2 cord coils
- [ ] lobster clasp
- [ ] chain-nose pliers (2 pair)
- [ ] sharp scissors
- [ ] tape measure or ruler
- [ ] craft glue

To make the Bracelet:

Always apply craft glue to cut cord ends and allow to dry.

1. Measure your wrist and decide how loose you want your bracelet. This is your finshed bracelet size. Cut a piece of paracord this length, minus the clasp length.

2. Apply a small amount of glue to one cord end. Insert the end into 1 cord coil and allow to dry.

3. Slide the beads on the cord. Repeat Step 2 to finish the remaining cord end.

4. Follow Opening and Closing A Cord Coil Loop (below) to attach the lobster clasp to one cord coil.

Opening and Closing A Cord Coil Loop

Hold one side of the cord coil loop with the chain-nose pliers. With a second pair of chain-nose pliers, gently hold the other side of the loop. Open the loop by pulling one pair of pliers toward you while pushing the other away.

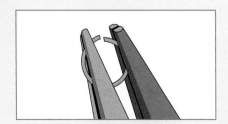

Close the loop by pushing and pulling the pliers in opposite directions, bringing the ends back together.

Bottle Holder

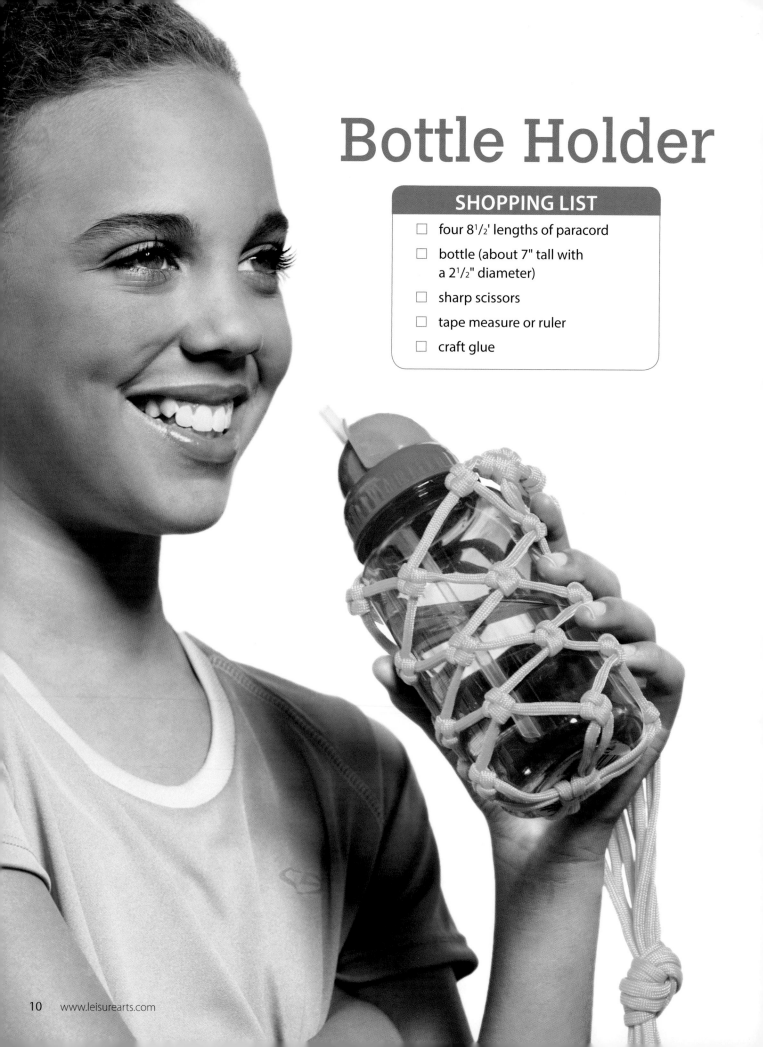

To make the Bottle Holder:

Always apply craft glue to cut cord ends and allow to dry.

1. For the center bottom knot, cross the cords at the center *(Fig. 1)*, being sure the horizontal cords are on top.

Fig. 1

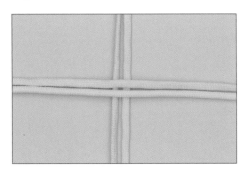

2. Fold the top ends of the vertical cords down and the bottom ends up *(Fig. 2)*.

Fig. 2

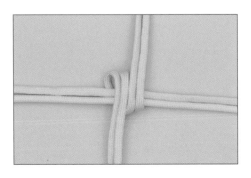

3. Fold the right ends of the horizontal cords to the left, over the right vertical cords, and through the loop of the left vertical cords *(Fig. 3)*. Fold the left end of the horizontal cords to the right, over the left vertical cords, and through the loop of the right vertical cords *(Fig. 4)*. Holding the knot, tighten and adjust the cords to form a square *(Fig. 5)*.

Fig. 3

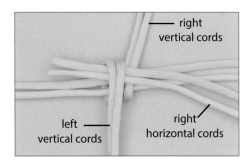

Fig. 4

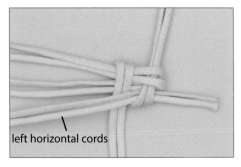

Fig. 5

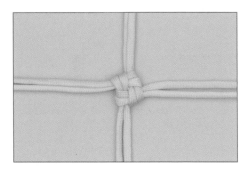

4. For the first Cross Knot, use one set of cords from the center bottom knot. Make an "S" shape with the right cord, over and under the left cord *(Fig. 6)*.

Fig. 6

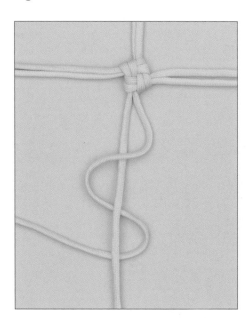

5. Bring the left cord under the "S" and through the loop at the top of the "S" (Fig. 7). Bring the left cord through the bottom of the "S" (Fig. 8).

Fig. 7

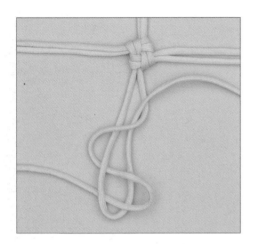

Fig. 8

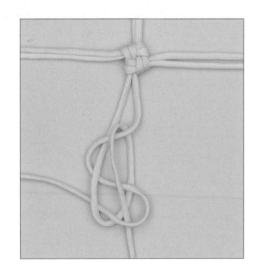

6. Holding the knot, tighten and adjust the cords to form a Cross Knot about 1¼" from the center bottom knot (Fig. 9).

Fig. 9

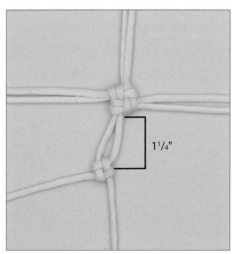

7. Repeat Steps 4-5 with the remaining cords to tie 3 more Cross Knots (Fig. 10).

Fig. 10

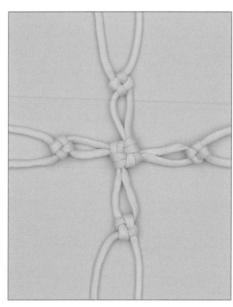

8. Taking a cord from 2 adjacent knots, repeat Steps 4-5 to tie a Cross Knot (Figs. 11-12). Tie 3 more Cross Knots around the center knots.

Fig. 11

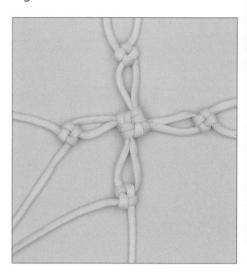

Fig. 12

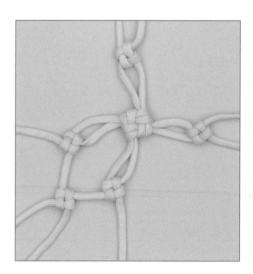

9. Always using adjacent cords, continue to tie rounds of Cross Knots (about 1" apart) until the bottle holder is about 7½" long *(Fig. 13)*.

Fig. 13

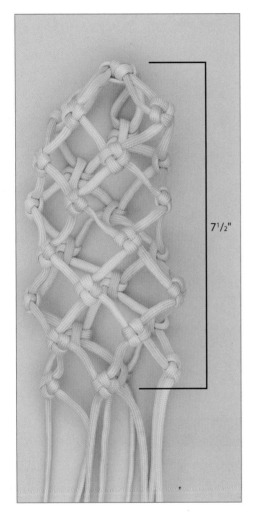

7½"

10. For the straps, use both cords from 2 adjacent knots held together as one and repeat Steps 4-5 to tie a Cross Knot about 1" from the last row of knots *(Fig. 14)*. Make 2 more Cross Knots *(Fig. 15)*. Repeat on the other side.

Fig. 14

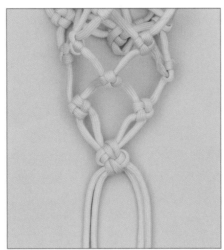

Fig. 15

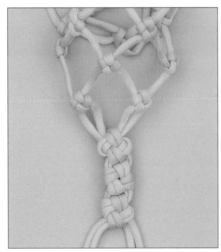

11. Tie all 8 cords together with an Overhand Knot (page 22) about 8" from the last Cross Knots. Trim the cord ends about 3" from the knot and apply a generous amount of craft glue to the ends.

Rhinestones & Paracord Bracelet

SHOPPING LIST

- ☐ 24" length of paracord
- ☐ 4" length of rhinestone chain
- ☐ friendship thread
- ☐ side-release buckle
- ☐ two large-eye hand sewing needles
- ☐ sharp scissors
- ☐ tape measure or ruler
- ☐ craft glue
- ☐ masking, painter's, or duct tape

To make the Bracelet:

Always apply craft glue to cut cord ends and allow to dry.

1. Measure your wrist and decide how loose you want your bracelet; add 1¹/₂". Cut 2 paracord lengths this measurement.

2. Insert about 1" of each cord through one buckle piece from front to back. Secure the ends to the cords with narrow pieces of tape. Repeat with remaining ends and buckle piece *(Fig. 1)*. Tape down both buckles.

Fig. 1

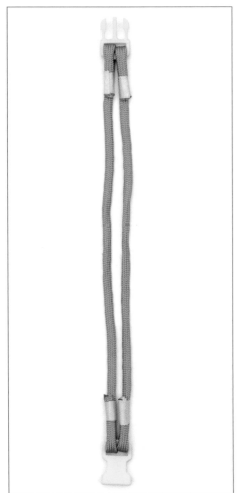

3. Thread each needle with a 24" length of friendship thread; knot one end. About 1" below one buckle piece, sew through the paracord with one needle from each side forming an "X".

4. Center the rhinestone chain between the paracord lengths.

5. Wrap the right friendship thread strand around the chain below the first rhinestone *(Fig. 2)*.

6. Wrap the left friendship thread strand around the chain below the first rhinestone *(Fig. 3)*.

7. Repeat Steps 5-6 *(Fig. 4)* along the length of the rhinestone chain.

8. After the last rhinestone, insert the needles through the paracord forming an "X". Wrap the thread ends around the cords once and tie in a knot; trim the ends.

9. Cut two 16" lengths of friendship thread. Beginning just below the buckle and leaving a 4" tail, wrap one thread length around the cords for about ³/₄". Tie the ends into a knot on the wrong side. Apply glue to the knot and allow to dry. Trim the ends close to the knot. Repeat on the remaining end of the bracelet.

Fig. 2

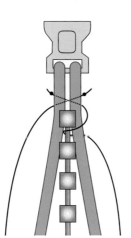

Fig. 3

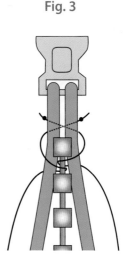

Fig. 4

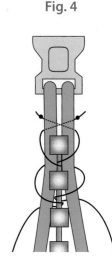

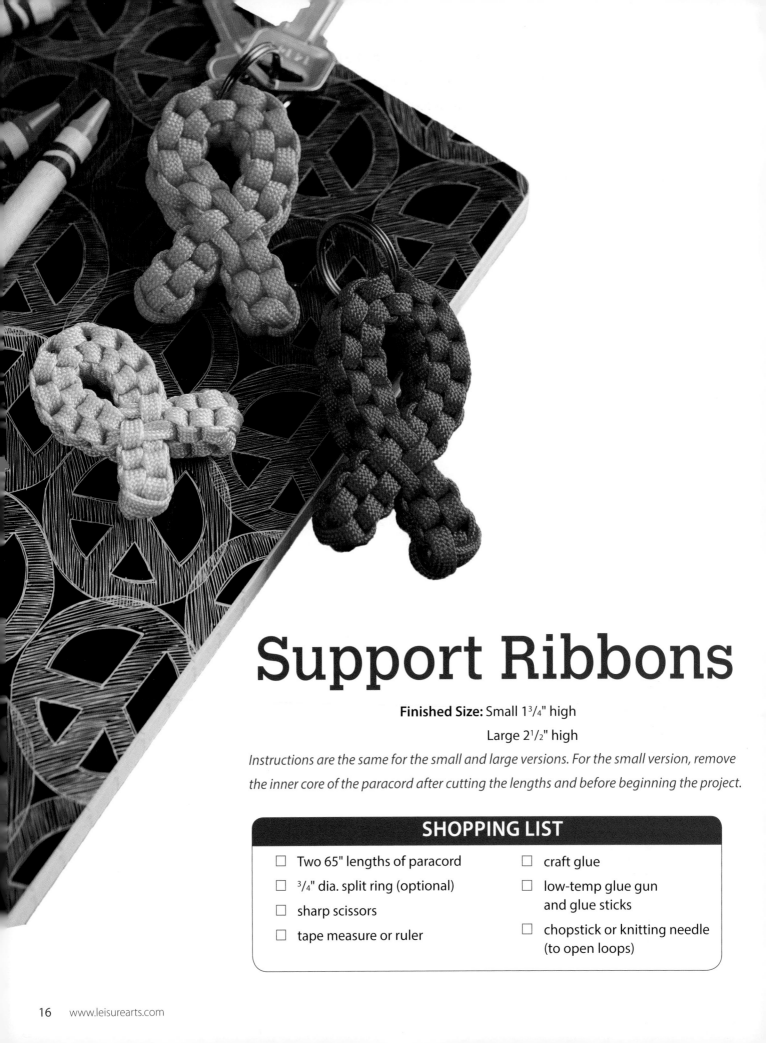

Support Ribbons

Finished Size: Small 1³/₄" high

Large 2¹/₂" high

Instructions are the same for the small and large versions. For the small version, remove the inner core of the paracord after cutting the lengths and before beginning the project.

SHOPPING LIST

- ☐ Two 65" lengths of paracord
- ☐ ³/₄" dia. split ring (optional)
- ☐ sharp scissors
- ☐ tape measure or ruler
- ☐ craft glue
- ☐ low-temp glue gun and glue sticks
- ☐ chopstick or knitting needle (to open loops)

To make the Ribbon:

Always apply craft glue to cut cord ends and allow to dry.

1. With the horizontal cord on top, cross the cords at the center *(Fig. 1)*.

Fig. 1

2. Fold the top end of the vertical cord down and the bottom end up *(Fig. 2)*.

Fig. 2

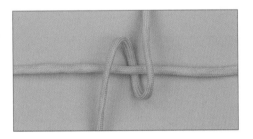

3. Fold the right end of the horizontal cord to the left, over the right vertical cord, and under the left vertical cord *(Fig. 3)*.

Fig. 3

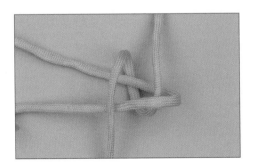

4. Fold the left end of the horizontal cord to the right, over the left vertical cord, and under the right vertical cord *(Fig. 4)*.

Fig. 4

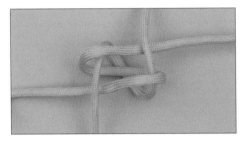

5. Alternately pull the vertical and horizontal cord ends until a tight square forms *(Figs. 5-6)*.

Fig. 5

Fig. 6

6. Repeat Steps 2-5 until you have 15 knots. Slide the split ring on 2 cords *(Fig. 7)*. Being careful to catch the ring in the knot, tie 1 knot *(Fig. 8)*. Continue tying until you have a total of 25 knots.

Fig. 7

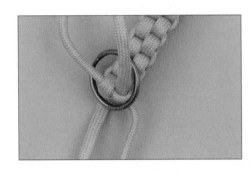

Fig. 8

7. Fold the ribbon at the ring or at knot #16, if you are not using a ring. Use your chopstick or knitting needle to open the #6 and #7 loops *(Fig. 9)*.

Fig. 9

8. Bring the top cord end through the opened #7 loop *(Fig. 10)*. Bring the bottom cord end through the opened #6 loop *(Fig. 11)*. Pull to tighten both cords.

Fig. 10

Fig. 11

9. Flip the ribbon over and repeat Steps 7-8 to thread the remaining two cord ends through the #6 and #7 loops on this side *(Fig. 12)*.

Fig. 12

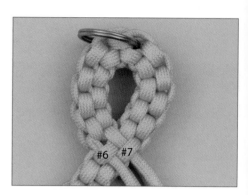

10. Position the cord ends as shown in **Fig. 13** and repeat Steps 2-5 to tie 5 more knots.

Fig.13

11. Use the glue gun to apply glue to each cord close to the last knot; allow to cool. Cut the cords close to the last knot and apply more glue; allow to cool.

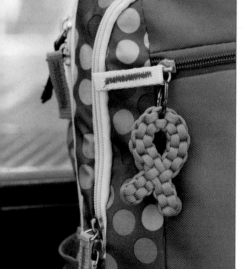

Para-Bead Jewelry

Bracelet shown on page 20.

SHOPPING LIST

Bracelet

- [ ] 54" length of paracord (bracelet and 1 end bead)
- [ ] 18" length *each* of 5 colors of paracord (beads)
- [ ] sharp scissors
- [ ] tape measure or ruler
- [ ] craft glue
- [ ] low-temp glue gun and glue sticks

Necklace

- [ ] 84" length of paracord (necklace and 1 end bead)
- [ ] five 18" lengths of assorted colors of paracord (5 beads)
- [ ] sharp scissors
- [ ] tape measure or ruler
- [ ] craft glue
- [ ] low-temp glue gun and glue sticks

3. For the end bead, use the 18" bracelet cord length and refer to Paracord Beads (page 24) to make a bead near the folded end of the bracelet *(Fig. 2)*. For the middle beads, use the remaining 18" cord lengths to make a total of 5 beads on the center of the bracelet *(Fig. 3)*.

Fig. 2

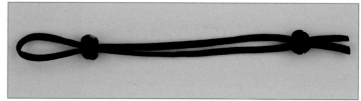

Fig. 3

To make the Bracelet:

Always apply craft glue to cut cord ends and allow to dry.

1. Cut an 18" length of bracelet cord for the end bead and set aside. Measure your wrist and decide how loose you want your bracelet. This is your finished bracelet size. Cut a length of bracelet cord **twice** this measurement plus 18".

2. Fold the bracelet cord in half and tie a Diamond Knot (page 23) at your finished bracelet size *(Fig. 1)*. Trim the cord ends to about ¹/₂"- ³/₄".

4. To close the bracelet, slip the loop over the Diamond Knot and cinch with the end bead on the bracelet *(Fig. 4)*.

Fig. 4

Fig. 1

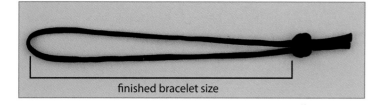

finished bracelet size

To make the Necklace:

Always apply craft glue to cut cord ends and allow to dry.

1. Cut a 66" and an 18" length of necklace cord. Set the 18" length aside for the bead.

2. Fold the 66" cord in half and tie a Diamond Knot (page 23) about 23" from the folded end. Trim the cord ends to about 1½" *(Fig. 5)*.

Fig. 5

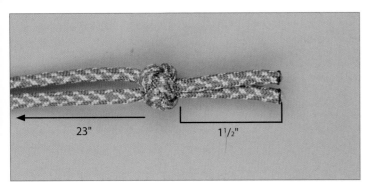

3. For the end bead, use the 18" necklace cord length and refer to Paracord Beads (page 24) to make a bead near the folded end of the necklace *(Fig. 6)*.

Fig. 6

4. For the middle beads, use the remaining 18" cord lengths to make a total of 5 beads on the center of the necklace*(Fig. 7)*.

Fig. 7

5. To close the necklace, slip the loop over the Diamond Knot and cinch with the end bead on the necklace *(Fig. 8)*.

Fig. 8

21

General Instructions

Cobra Stitch Knot

1. Follow **Fig. 1** to tie the first half of a Cobra Stitch Knot, pulling the cords to tighten.

Fig. 1

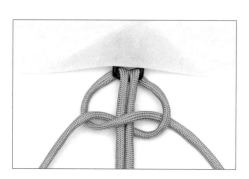

2. Follow **Fig. 2** to tie the second half of a Cobra Stitch Knot, pulling the cords to tighten.

Fig. 2

Finishing The Ends

1. On the wrong side, thread the cord ends under the last knot *(Fig. 3)*; tighten.

Fig. 3

2. Trim the cords, leaving about 1/4" tails *(Fig. 4)*. Apply a generous amount of craft glue to the cord ends and allow to dry.

Fig. 4

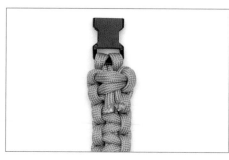

Overhand Knot

An Overhand Knot tied with a single cord *(Fig. 5)* can be a stop for beads or a decorative finish for the cord end.

Fig. 5

An Overhand Knot tied with multiple cords *(Fig. 6)* is often used at the beginning or end of a project.

Fig. 6

We have made every effort to ensure that these instructions are accurate and complete. We cannot, however, be responsible for human error, typographical mistakes, or variations in individual work.

Production Team: Designer - Kelly Reider; Technical Writer - Jean Lewis; Technical Associate - Mary Hutcheson; Editorial Writer - Susan Frantz Wiles; Senior Graphic Artist - Lora Puls; Photostylist - Lori Wenger; Photographers - Jason Masters and Ken West.

Diamond Knot

Two different cord colors are shown for clarity. For a project using only one color of cord, it may be helpful to mark your cords left and right with small pieces of tape.

1. Hold the cord ends on either side of your middle finger *(Fig. 7)* at the measurement given in your project instructions.

Fig. 7

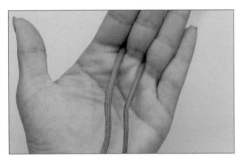

2. Make a "P" with the left (shown in purple) cord *(Fig. 8)*. Make a loop under the "P" with the right (shown in pink) cord *(Fig. 9)*.

Fig. 8

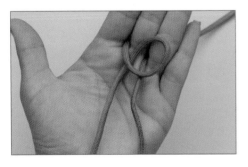

Fig. 9

3. Bring the right (pink) cord over the "P", under itself, and over the "P" *(Fig. 10)*. The knot should have loops on either side and an open diamond in the center.

Fig. 10

4. Bring the left (purple) cord around the right side of the knot, under all the cords and up through the center of the diamond *(Fig. 11)*.

Fig. 11

5. Bring the right (pink) cord around the top of the knot, under all the cords on the left side and up through the center of the diamond *(Fig. 12)*.

Fig. 12

6. Holding the cord ends and the cords on the project end, gently pull to tighten the knot *(Figs. 13-14)*. **Tip:** As you pull, adjust the loops in the knot to keep a round shape.

Fig. 13

Fig. 14

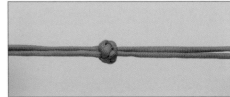

Paracord Beads

Paracord beads, also known as ranger beads, are tied with a single length of cord around a core of two cords. A single bead can be used as an end bead on a necklace or bracelet or can be simply decorative.

1. Leaving about a 3" tail at the top *(Fig. 15)*, wrap the long cord end around the core cords as shown in **Figs. 16-17.**

Fig. 15

Fig. 16

Fig. 17

2. Insert the long cord end through the left loop *(Fig. 18)*.

Fig. 18

3. Turn your work over *(Fig. 19)*.

Fig. 19

4. Insert the left loop into the right loop, creating a new loop *(Fig. 20)*.

Fig. 20

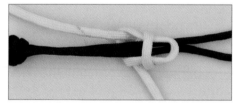

5. Insert the long cord through the new loop created in Step 4 *(Fig. 21)*.

Fig. 21

6. Slightly tighten the knot by pulling on the long and short cord ends *(Fig. 22)*.

Fig. 22

7. Insert the short cord under the "X" (indicated by the red lines) from right to left *(Fig. 23)*.

Fig. 23

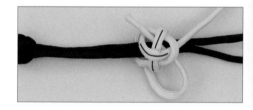

8. Tighten the knot by pulling on the long and short cord ends *(Fig. 24)*.

Fig. 24

9. Use the glue gun to apply glue to the cords, close to the knot; allow to cool. Trim the cord ends close to the knot and apply a generous amount of glue to the cut ends.